Jatrean Sanders Enterprises, Incorporated
P.O. Box 28660
Atlanta, GA 30358 jatrean@jatreansanders.com

Purchasing Information:
www.jatreansanders.com

ISBN:978-0-578-85753-4
First Printing, USA

This book is dedicated to
an Eternal God who made my
childhood dreams a reality,

My Parents,
whose belief in me is endless and knows no bounds,

My Little "Big" Sister,
who is the pea in my pod,

and
My Rock
and his Son,
who inspired this story.

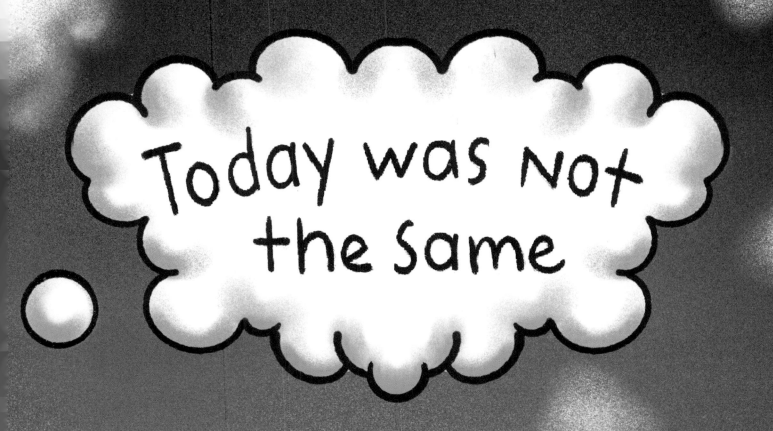

Today was not the Same

By: Jatrean Marie Sanders, Esq.

Illustrated by Tim Furlow

Jatrean Sanders Enterprises, Inc.
Published in Atlanta, GA, USA

When I woke up this morning,
today felt very strange.
I could not figure out why,
but today was not the same.

Normally, my parents wake me up
with a tickle and a laugh.
But this morning when they came in my room,
they both seemed very sad.

I looked them in their eyes
and asked them what was wrong.
My parents grabbed me tightly
and held me very long.

I started getting dressed that day
to head off to school.
But when I came downstairs,
my parents were breaking the "no-tv rule."
They both stood in front of the tv
holding each other's hand.
As the man on the news talked,
my mom said, "When will this end?"

My parents both took me to school,
which has never happened before.
My dad said, "Let's pray
before we walk out the door."

When I arrived at the schoolhouse,
the day felt very strange.
I could not figure out why,
but today was not the same.

Ms. Hudson and Ms. Williams
went to a corner to cry.
But Ms. Wilson and Mr. Smith
chatted casually as they walked by.

After school, I waited for the bus,
but my grandmother arrived instead.
I ran to the car in excitement
and she jumped out to kiss my head.
"Granny, what are you doing here,
I normally ride the bus."
"I wanted to see my grandbaby
and share the afternoon – just us."

When we pulled up at my house,
the day felt very strange.
I could not figure out why,
but today was not the same.

As I sat doing my homework,
Granny cooked and cooked.
I said, "If you keep cooking,
we'll have food everywhere you look!"

Granny laughed and smiled,
then kissed me on my head.
She said to me, "Oh, little one,
I have to make sure you're fed.
See, feeding you the food I've cooked,
even when I'm gone,
is the way I love you
and keep your body strong."

"But Granny, I eat my vegetables
and I'm super strong."
Granny said, "No not that strength,
the strength to carry on."

"The strength to fight injustice,
racism and hate.
The strength to prove again and again
that being Black makes you great.
The strength to open doors
when they're closed in your face.
The strength to run harder and faster
just to win the same life-race.
The strength to go to work or school,
and smile or laugh and grin.
Even though you're being judged
because of the color of your skin."

As I listened to Granny
I started to feel strange.
I could not figure out why,
but I did not feel the same.

After dinner I took a bath,
and prepared to go to sleep.
But downstairs I could hear loud sounds
and stomping of feet.

I tipped down the stairs quietly
and heard loud voices too.

I heard Mom say, "A peaceful protest
is what we all should do."
Then Dad said, "No, not this time,
marching alone won't get us through."

Grandad said, "You want more of us to march and go to jail?"

Dad said, "Yes,
if we want justice to prevail."

Granny said, "I agree,
thousands marched after King died.
If we had not done so,
segregation would be alive."

1968

2020

Auntie said, "There's no right answer to any part of this. We just want to love, prosper and be able to coexist."

Dad yelled, "Coexist! I want to do more than that . . . I want to face an officer without being hurt or attacked."

"What!?" I said aloud. "Why would the police hurt you? Police only stop bad guys and arrest criminals too."

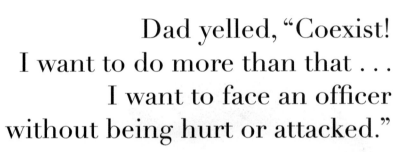

"Well, my child," my dad said,
as he wiped away my tears.
"What I'm about to tell you
may be well beyond your years."

"Some police — not all —
fear you because of the color of your skin.
They assume you have done wrong
before the investigation begins."

"So, when they pull a Black man over,
or they arrive at a scene,
they may treat that Black man differently,
hurt him or even scream."

My mom said, "It's not just men . . .
it happens to Black women too.
We wish we didn't have to tell you this,
but unfortunately, it's all true."

Granny said, "The police attacked
a Black man the other day.
They hurt him so badly,
he later passed away."

"The police said the man fought back,
they said they were in fear.
But when they searched his body,
no weapon was close or near."

I feel it now, deep in my heart
this all feels very strange.
I now know why in my heart
today is not the same.

"I want to see HIS face," I asked.
"I want to know HER name.
Even though we're all different,
we're actually all the same."

"If this could happen to this man or woman,
it could happen to any of us.
What are we supposed to do
when the police we're told to trust?"

"You're absolutely right my child,"
my mom said to me.
"But you should never fear
what may never be."

"We will teach you what to do
if you run into the law.
And we will fight to change the rules
that are in place thus far."

"We must also vote to get new leaders
who will advocate for change.
Because we cannot survive and thrive
if things simply stay the same."

As I listened to my family,
I started to feel less strange.
I'm happy they told me why
today did not feel the same.

I will pray hard tonight for those
Black and Brown lives that were lost.
And pray hard for those that hate
my skin color at any cost.

I will also pray for new leaders,
protestors, and allies all the same.
Because each of them simply wants
America to change.

When I woke up early this morning,
today felt very strange.
But as I go to bed tonight,
I'm believing tomorrow will bring *change.*

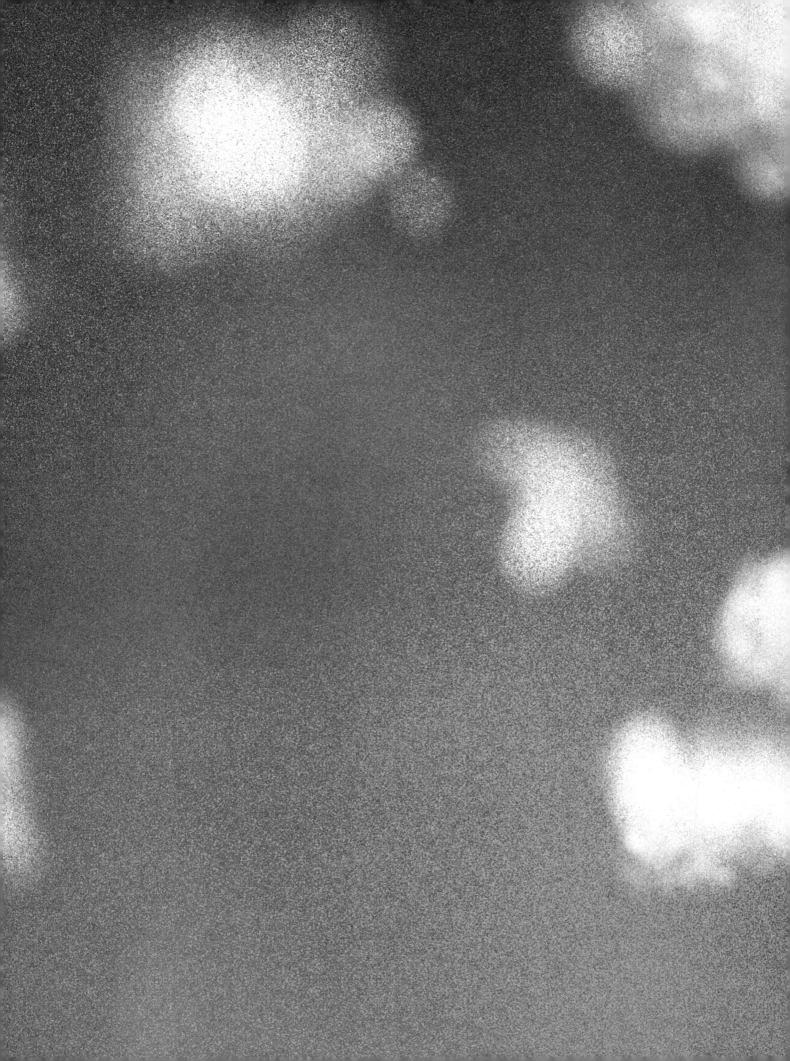